STARTING TOGETHER

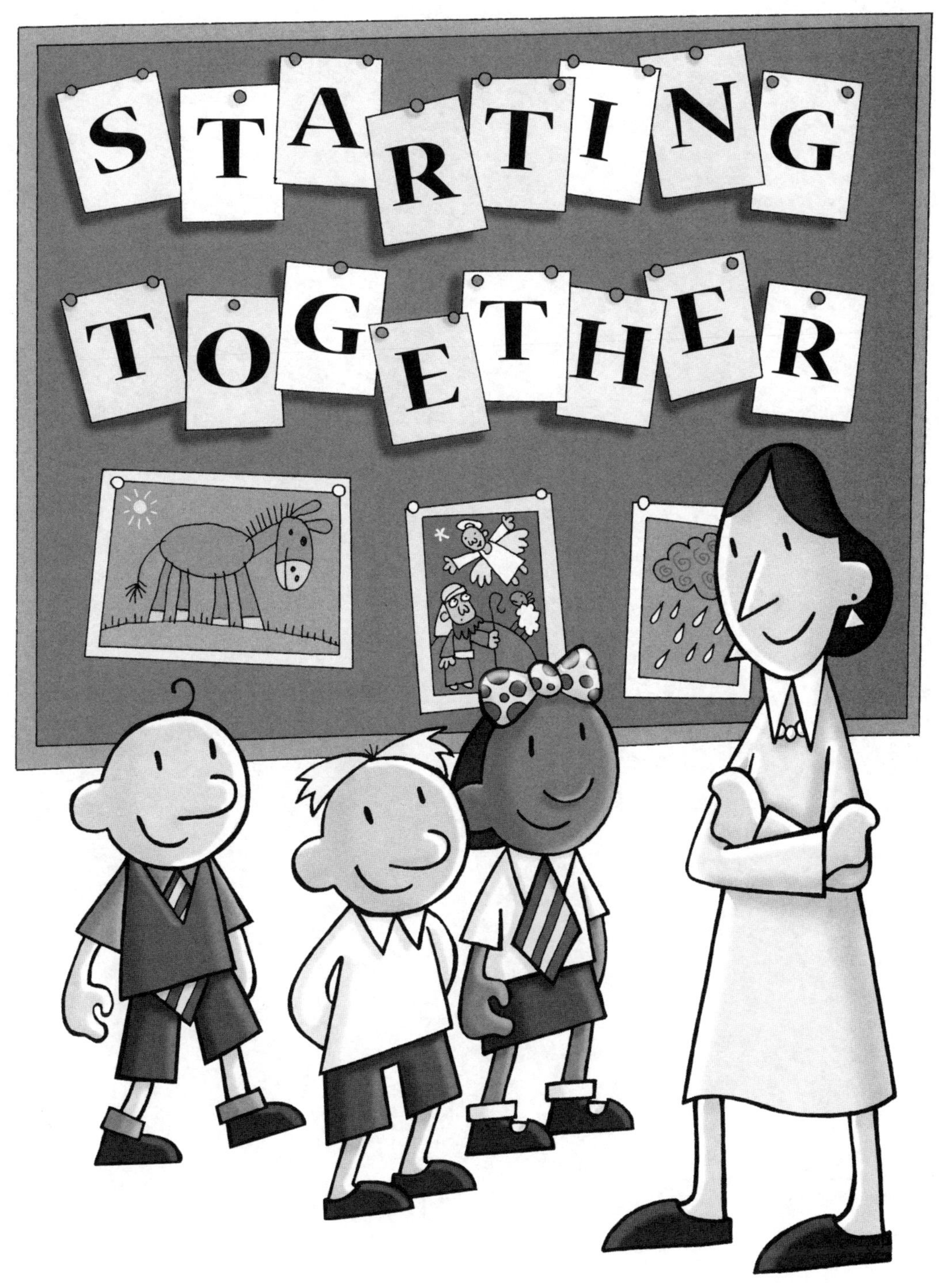

Brian Ogden

24 assembly stories for Early Learners

Published by
The Bible Reading Fellowship
First Floor, Elsfield Hall
15–17 Elsfield Way, Oxford OX2 8FG

ISBN 1 84101 257 2
First published 2003
10 9 8 7 6 5 4 3 2 1 0

Acknowledgments
Scripture quotations are from the Contemporary English Version © American Bible Society 1991, 1992, 1995. Used by permission/Anglicisations © British and Foreign Bible Society 1997.

A catalogue record for this book is available from the British Library

Printed and bound in Malta

Contents

Foreword

When I first read Brian Ogden's stories about Mrs Jolley and her class of children, I knew they would be an instant success. Brian has a great understanding of young children, situations and topics which are relevant to school life (although I did manage to correct him once or twice!). When the *On the Story Mat* series was first published, I was a busy Deputy Headteacher of an Infant and Nursery School and led regular assemblies, so the stories were a valuable resource. Children could quickly identify with the characters of Daisy Hill Primary School and also with the characters from the Bible. In fact, my class liked the stories so much that they would often ask for them to be read at other times too!

Starting Together is an excellent resource for school assemblies in the Foundation Stage and Key Stage One. The themes are meaningful, they can be expanded upon easily and can be used as a stimulus for discussion. Brian writes with sensitivity, and his touches of humour amuse all ages. The illustrations will appeal to the children and can be turned into overheads to use as visual aids. During collective worship, children can reflect upon the theme as they join in with the prayers. The stories could also be used as part of the RE curriculum and as a stimulus for Circle Times.

I know that you and your children will enjoy the stories as much as we have. Thank you, Brian, and please keep writing!

Gill Grainger

Introduction

This book contains material for twenty-four assemblies. The stories originally appeared in the *On the Story Mat* series of six books. Here they have been placed under four headings for easy reference: *Me*, *Me and you*, *Others* and *Festivals*. Each assembly contains the theme, aim, Bible reference and short Bible passage, a photocopiable illustration, a story and a closing 'join-in' prayer.

The stories are set in the Reception class of Daisy Hill Primary School. As in any similar situation, the story mat is an important feature in the classroom. The teacher, Mrs Jolley, relates the various everyday happenings in the classroom to stories from the Bible. There are stories from both the Old and the New Testament. The prayers at the end of each story are all 'join-in' prayers with very simple responses for the children.

You will readily relate to the children, their teacher and the incidents that occur in Mrs Jolley's classroom. It could be yours! Although set in a Reception class, the stories have been used successfully throughout Key Stage One.

ME

These five assemblies consider the 'me-centred' characteristic of young children—- starting in school, changing schools, going to hospital and so on. Each story starts with a frequently found situation.

 **Theme**

The first few days in school can be hard for both children and their parents. It wasn't easy for Hannah or Samuel to be separated from one another, but God helped them both.

 **Aim**

To help children to settle into school

 **Bible reference**

1 Samuel 1:1—2:10
When it was the time of year to go to Shiloh again, Hannah and Elkanah took Samuel to the Lord's house. They brought the little boy to Eli. 'Sir,' Hannah said, 'a few years ago I stood here beside you and asked the Lord to give me a child. Here he is! The Lord gave me just what I asked for. Now I am giving him to the Lord, and he will be the Lord's servant for as long as he lives.'
1 SAMUEL 1:24–28

A join-in prayer

Father of all,
For mums and dads and those who care for us,
Thank you.
For their love for us,
Thank you.
For all that they do for us,
Thank you.
For our homes and families,
Thank you.

1

I want my mum

It was Monday morning in Mrs Jolley's Reception class. And it was a very noisy Monday morning.

Most of the children were looking at books. David, Joshua and Sarah had some big picture books. Emma, Hannah and Michael were playing a word game. They were all working quietly and happily.

The noise was coming from Sam. Sam was not happy. Sam was crying and Sam was shouting.

Mrs Jolley put her arm round Sam. Mrs Jolley tried to stop Sam from crying and shouting.

'I want my mummy!' shouted Sam.

'I want to go home!' shouted Sam.

The tears rolled down Sam's face on to Mrs Jolley's arm. Mrs Jolley wiped Sam's tears with a tissue.

After a long time, Sam stopped crying and shouting. Sam just sat and sniffed.

'Time for a story, everyone,' said Mrs Jolley. The children came and sat on the story mat. Sam sat next to David. David put his arm round Sam.

'Sometimes we miss our mums when we start school,' said Mrs Jolley. 'I'm going to tell you a story about a boy called Samuel.

'Samuel's mummy was called Hannah and his father's name was Elkanah. For a long time Hannah couldn't have any children. Hannah went to God's house and prayed. She prayed that God would let her have a baby.

'God heard her prayers and baby Samuel was born. Hannah and Elkanah were very happy and thanked God for their baby.

'One day, Hannah took Samuel to God's house. Hannah spoke to the priest at God's house. The priest's name was Eli.

'"God gave me Samuel," said Hannah. "I promised God that I would bring Samuel to you when he was old enough."

'Samuel stayed with Eli and helped Eli to look after God's house. Every year Hannah came to visit Samuel. Hannah brought him new clothes each time she came. Hannah and Elkanah had more children.

'Samuel grew up to be very special,' said Mrs Jolley.

'He must have been very brave,' said David, 'to leave his mummy.'

'He was, and so is our Sam,' said Mrs Jolley.

And David and Sam went off to play.

Theme

Children can very easily feel lost. Being separated from parents or from friends, even for a short time, can be distressing.

Aim

To give the assurance that we're never really lost

Bible reference

Luke 15:1–7

'If any of you has a hundred sheep, and one of them gets lost, what will you do? Won't you leave the ninety-nine in the field and go and look for the lost sheep until you find it? And when you find it, you will be so glad that you will put it on your shoulder and carry it home.'

LUKE 15:4–5

A join-in prayer

Father of all,
For those who work
in the police,
Thank you.
For those who work
on lifeboats,
Thank you.
For those who drive
ambulances,
Thank you.
For all who help
to keep us safe,
Thank you.

2

Lost and found

Mrs Jolley and the children went on a trip to a supermarket. Michael's mummy went with them.

They saw where the bread was made. They saw where all the lorries unloaded the boxes. They saw the big freezers with the lollies and ice cream. They saw the shelves being filled with crisps.

When it was time to go back to school, they couldn't see James.

'Oh dear,' said Mrs Jolley. 'We shall have to look for him.'

Michael's mummy went to look for James. After a few minutes, James came back with Michael's mummy.

'James was looking at the lollies in the big freezer,' said Michael's mummy.

Everybody went back to school. The children sat on the story mat.

'I'm going to tell you a story that Jesus told about being lost,' said Mrs Jolley. 'One day a shepherd counted his sheep.

'"Ninety-five, ninety-six, ninety-seven, ninety-eight, ninety-nine, er..." he counted. "Oh dear," he said. "One is missing."

'Off went the shepherd to find his sheep. He looked in the fields. The sheep wasn't there. He looked in the woods. The sheep wasn't there. The shepherd looked in the hills. There, in a deep hole, he found the sheep.

'He put the sheep on his shoulders. He carried the sheep home.

'The shepherd was very happy he had found the sheep. The other sheep were very happy their friend had been found. The shepherd had a party to show how happy he was.

'I think the sheep had a party too,' said Mrs Jolley.

'James got lost and then he was found,' said Emma.

'Can we have a party, please, Mrs Jolley?' asked all the children.

 **Theme**

Both home and school can do much to prepare children for a visit to hospital.

 **Aim**

To show that hospitals are not places to be feared

 **Bible reference**

2 Kings 5:1–19

Naaman walked down to the Jordan; he waded out into the water and stooped down in it seven times, just as Elisha had told him. Straight away, he was cured, and his skin became as smooth as a child's. Naaman and his officials went back to Elisha. Naaman stood in front of him and announced, 'Now I know that the God of Israel is the only God in the whole world.'

2 KINGS 5:14–15

A join-in prayer

Loving Father,
We pray for all people
who are not well,
Please be with them.
We pray for doctors
and nurses,
Please be with them.
We pray for those who
cannot see or cannot
hear very well,
Please be with them.
We pray especially
today for...
Please be with them.

3

Emma and Naaman get better

Emma was not happy. Emma didn't play with her friend Hannah at playtime. She didn't eat her crisps and chocolate at dinner time.

Mrs Jolley spoke to Emma's mummy after school.

'Emma has to go into hospital,' said her mummy. 'She hasn't been able to hear very well and she has to have a grommet put in her ear. Emma is unhappy because she has to go to hospital.'

The next day, just before milk time, Mrs Jolley asked all the children to sit on the story mat. 'I'm going to tell you a story about a man called Naaman,' she said.

'Naaman was a soldier. Naaman was a very important soldier. But Naaman was very unhappy. He was unhappy because he was ill.

'He went to see Elisha. Elisha was a man who loved God. Elisha told Naaman to wash seven times in the river.

'Naaman thought this was silly and he was very angry. He thought people would laugh at him if he washed in the river. He didn't want to wash in the river. But he changed his mind and went to the river.

'He washed seven times in the river. When he came out, he was well again. Naaman the soldier was very happy.

'Sometimes,' said Mrs Jolley, 'we have to do things we don't want to do to make us better.'

Emma went into hospital the next day. Emma took a new teddy bear with her. She called the bear Naaman.

In a few days Emma was back at school again.

'I'm glad I went,' she said. 'It was nice in hospital. The nurses were fun and there were lots of toys. I feel much better now. And so does Naaman!'

Theme

'It's not fair!' Life is rarely fair, but it can help to consider those things we do have, rather than those we don't.

Aim

To think about what we do have, not what we don't have

Bible reference

Genesis 37

Jacob loved Joseph more than he did any of his other sons, because Joseph was born after Jacob was very old. Jacob had given Joseph a fine coat to show that he was his favourite son, and so Joseph's brothers hated him.

GENESIS 37:3–4

A join-in prayer

Loving Lord,
We have so many
good things.
When we say, 'It isn't fair',
We are sorry.
When we are jealous
of others,
We are sorry.
When we forget people
who have nothing,
We are sorry.
When we don't say,
'thank you',
We are sorry.

A coat for Joseph

'It's not fair,' said Sarah. 'Hannah's always playing with Emma. I never play with Emma.'

'It's not fair,' said Sam. 'Michael's got all the Man United strip. I've just got my brother's old things.'

'It's not fair,' said Rosie. 'Emma's got her own pony. All I've got's an old bike.'

'It's not fair,' said Nathan. 'David's going to America on holiday. We've got to stay at home.'

It seemed to be a 'not fair' day in Mrs Jolley's class. All the children were wishing they had what someone else had. Mrs Jolley heard them and asked them to sit on the story mat.

'It's not fair,' she said, smiling. 'Mrs Jones, next door, has got a lovely class of children... And so have I... really!

'I want to tell you a "not fair" story. It's a story about a man called Jacob. Jacob had twelve sons. Jacob loved all his sons. But Jacob loved one son more than the others. Jacob loved Joseph most of all.

'Jacob gave Joseph a special present. Jacob gave Joseph a special coat. Joseph loved his coat. Joseph wore his coat all the time. He wore it when it was hot. And he wore it when he was cold.

'The other brothers were very jealous of Joseph.

'"It's not fair," said Reuben. "Joseph's got a special coat."

'"It's not fair," said Judah.

'"It's not fair," said Benjamin.

'"It's not fair," said all the rest.

'One day all the brothers went off to look after the sheep. Only Joseph stayed at home.

'"Joseph," said Jacob, "I want you to go to see if your brothers and the sheep are all right."

'Joseph's brothers saw him coming. When Joseph arrived, they did a very nasty thing. They took off his special coat and tore it up. They threw Joseph down a deep hole. They sold Joseph to some men who were going to Egypt. They didn't think they would ever see Joseph again.

'This happened because Joseph's brothers said, "It isn't fair." They were jealous of Joseph. They were unkind to Joseph.

'Being jealous of someone can make us unkind to them,' said Mrs Jolley. 'Before you say, "It's not fair", think about all the things you *do* have.'

 **Theme**

The thought of a new school, so common today with a mobile population, can be frightening to children. Both old and new schools have a part to play in helping children to settle happily.

 **Aim**

To show that change is never easy but we soon get used to it

 **Bible reference**

Genesis 12:1–7

The Lord said to Abram: 'Leave your country, your family, and your relatives and go to the land that I will show you. I will bless you and make your descendants into a great nation. You will become famous and be a blessing to others.'

GENESIS 12:1–2

A join-in prayer

Dear Jesus,
You know what it is like to leave home.
You left heaven and came to earth.
You left Nazareth to start your work.
For families moving to new homes,
Please be with them.
For old people giving up their homes,
Please be with them.
For those who have lost their homes because of war,
Please be with them.

5

A new school for Nathan

Nathan's mummy came to see Mrs Jolley after school one day. Nathan played in the sand tray while his mummy and Mrs Jolley talked.

'I've come to tell you that we are moving,' said Nathan's mummy. 'Our new home is a long way away. Nathan will have to go to a new school near our new home.'

'I'm very sorry to hear that,' said Mrs Jolley. 'The children will be sorry too.'

'We have sold our house and we have to move very soon,' said Nathan's mummy.

'Don't want to go,' said Nathan in a loud voice. Nathan looked as if he was going to cry. Nathan went home with his mummy.

The next day, after break, Mrs Jolley asked the children to sit on the story mat.

'Yesterday,' she said, 'Nathan's mummy told me that the family is moving. Nathan will be leaving Daisy Hill and going to a new school. Nathan is sad about it and so are we. But sometimes we have to leave our friends and our homes and make new ones.

'I want to tell you a story about a man who left his friends and his home. His name was Abraham. His wife's name was Sarah. Abraham and Sarah didn't have any children at that time. They lived in a city called Haran.

'One day God spoke to Abraham. God told Abraham that he had to leave Haran. He had to leave his country. He had to leave his father's home. And he had to leave most of his relations.

'God told Abraham that he was going to a special land. The land was called Canaan. Abraham was seventy-five years old when he left. I don't think Nathan is quite that old!

'Abraham did what God wanted, and after a long journey they arrived in Canaan. Abraham had lots of adventures in Canaan. But all the time God was with him.

'It must have been very hard for Abraham to leave his home. I'm sure that Abraham sent messages back to his friends in Haran. It is hard for us to have to say goodbye to Nathan. Perhaps we can send some messages to him. And perhaps he will send some to us. Maybe we could write to his new school.

'Nathan, we know you will be very happy in your new school, but we shall miss you.'

All the children drew cards for Nathan. One by one, they came and gave him their cards. Nathan looked sad when school finished.

Very soon, Mrs Jolley's class had a postcard. It was from Nathan. Nathan told them he was happy in his new school.

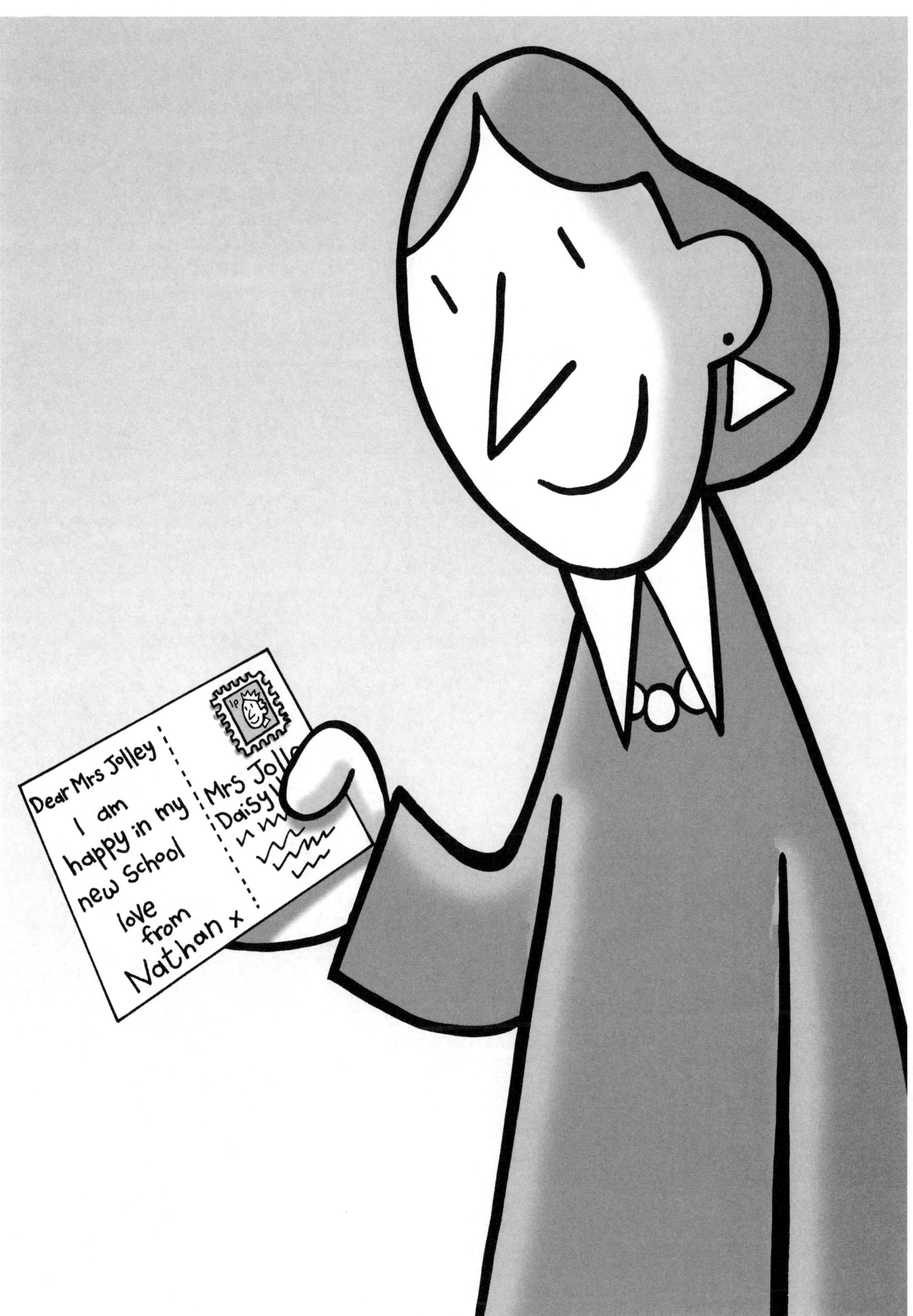
Dear Mrs Jolley
I am
happy in my
new School
love
from
Nathan x

ME AND YOU

The six stories in this section explore the relationship-building through which every child goes, with greater or lesser success. Themes include starting school, making friends, falling out and kindness to others.

 **Theme**

A new start can be easier for some than others, especially if friends are with them. Have you ever wondered what Jesus' disciples felt like when they had their new start?

 **Aim**

To help children to settle into school life

 **Bible reference**

Matthew 4:18–22

While Jesus was walking along the shore of Lake Galilee, he saw two brothers. One was Simon, also known as Peter, and the other was Andrew. They were fishermen, and they were casting their net into the lake. Jesus said to them, 'Come with me! I will teach you how to bring in people instead of fish.'

MATTHEW 4:18–19

A join-in prayer

Loving Father,
For our school and
our teachers,
Thank you.
For what we learn
at school,
Thank you.
For fun and friends,
Thank you.
For the friends of Jesus,
Thank you.

6

Starting together

It was the first day of term. Mrs Jolley had been very busy getting her classroom ready. The names of the new children were by their pegs. There were lots of lovely big pictures on the wall.

David and his mum were the first to arrive. David hung his coat on the peg with his name.

'See if you can find your name on one of the drawers,' said Mrs Jolley.

Soon the other new children arrived. Joshua came with his sister Rosie. Hannah and Emma walked in, holding hands. They were friends from play school. James came with Michael because they lived next door to each other. Sarah came with her dad.

'There you are, Sarah,' said her dad, 'I told you David would be here.' And Sarah sat at the same table as David.

There were so many things to choose that first morning. David chose to look at a picture book about cars, and Sarah found one about baby animals.

Later, Mrs Jolley asked all the children to go to one corner of the classroom. In the corner was a bright-coloured piece of carpet.

'This is our story mat,' said Mrs Jolley. 'Every day we shall come here for a special story. Today I want to tell you how Jesus found some new friends.

'Jesus was walking by the lakeside. It was a lovely day and the sun was shining on the big lake. Standing in the water with their fishing nets were two brothers. Their names were Simon and Andrew. They looked rather surprised when Jesus spoke to them.

'"Come with me," said Jesus. "I've got a special job for you to do."

'Further along the beach was a fishing boat. James and John were getting their boat ready to go out on the lake. They were going fishing in the deeper water. They looked rather surprised when Jesus spoke to them.

'"Come with me," said Jesus. "I've got a special job for you to do."

'Soon Jesus had twelve friends who went everywhere with him. These new friends quickly got to know each other. Each day they learned more and more from Jesus.'

Mrs Jolley looked at the children and smiled.

'You'll soon know each other and be friends. And there are lots and lots of things to learn together at school. And now it's playtime.'

 **Theme**

'Sorry' is a very hard word but one that is vital to learn. Balaam learns to admit he was wrong.

 **Aim**

To show the importance of saying 'sorry'

 **Bible reference**

Numbers 22:20–35
The angel said, 'You had no right to treat your donkey like that! I was the one who blocked your way, because I don't think you should go to Moab.' Balaam replied, 'I was wrong.'
NUMBERS 22:32, 34

A join-in prayer

Loving Father,
When we do or say wrong things,
We are sorry.
When we are unkind to our friends,
We are sorry.
When we are cross and lose our tempers,
We are sorry.
When we want our own way and sulk when we don't get it,
We are sorry.

7

Sometimes the donkey is right

It was time to go home. It had been a wet day. It was still raining when the children went to get their coats.

Sarah's coat and Joshua's coat were next to each other. The children kept their wellies on the floor under their coats. Sarah's wellies were red. Joshua's wellies were the same colour.

Sarah stood on one foot and put on her red wellies. Joshua looked for his wellies. They were not there.

'Sarah's wearing my wellies,' said Joshua.

'I'm not,' said Sarah. 'These are mine.'

'No, they're not,' shouted Joshua.

'Yes, they are,' Sarah shouted back.

Mrs Jolley took Sarah and Joshua back into the classroom.

'Now, let's see who these wellies belong to,' said Mrs Jolley. 'Take one off, please, Sarah.' Mrs Jolley looked at the name in the welly.

'Joshua, you are wrong,' said Mrs Jolley. 'These wellies have Sarah's name in them. Are you sure you wore your wellies to school today?'

Joshua thought about it.

'No, Mrs Jolley,' he said. 'I remember now, I didn't.'

The next morning Mrs Jolley asked the children to sit down on the story mat. 'Sometimes,' she said, 'we make a mistake.

'I'm going to tell you a story about a man and a donkey. The man's name was Balaam. We don't know the donkey's name.

'Balaam was riding along the road on his donkey. The donkey suddenly left the road and went into a field. Balaam got cross with the donkey.

'They went on and the donkey stopped by a wall. Balaam's leg was squashed against the wall. Balaam got even more cross with the donkey.

'They went on again and the donkey stopped and lay down. Balaam hit the donkey with his stick.

'The donkey stopped because it had seen an angel. Now God let Balaam see the angel. Balaam was very sorry he had got cross with his donkey.

'"You were right," Balaam said, "and I was wrong. I am very sorry I got cross."

'Sometimes,' said Mrs Jolley, 'we think we're right when we're not. Then we must say "sorry".'

Sarah and Joshua were soon friends again.

 **Theme**

Friendship can make heavy demands. True friends are there when they are needed.

 **Aim**

To show that being friends means a willingness to help

 **Bible reference**

Luke 5:17–26

God had given Jesus the power to heal the sick, and some people came carrying a crippled man on a mat. They tried to take him inside the house and put him in front of Jesus. But because of the crowd, they could not get him to Jesus. So they went up on the roof, where they removed some tiles and let the mat down in the middle of the room. When Jesus saw how much faith they had, he said to the crippled man, 'My friend, your sins are forgiven.'

LUKE 5:17b–20

A join-in prayer

Lord God,
Thank you for our friends.
For the fun we have
with our friends,
Thank you.
For all that we can share
with our friends,
Thank you.
For the help our friends
give us,
Thank you.
For all that they mean to us,
Thank you.

8

Best friends

David and Joshua were sitting in the playhouse. They were looking at a picture book together.

'You're my best friend,' said David.

'And you're my best friend too,' said Joshua.

Mrs Jolley heard the boys talking and smiled.

Emma and Hannah were playing in the sand tray.

'Will you be my best friend?' asked Emma.

'Yes, please,' said Hannah, 'and you're my best friend.'

Mrs Jolley heard what the girls said to each other and smiled.

A little later, Mrs Jolley spoke to all the children. 'It's time for our story. Come and sit on the story mat, please.'

David sat next to Joshua, and Emma sat next to Hannah.

'I'm going to tell you a story about friends. Friends are very special people. Friends sometimes do very special things for us.

'One day Jesus was in a house. Jesus was talking to a big crowd of people. There were people everywhere.

'There were people sitting on the chairs. There were people sitting on the floor. There were people looking in through the doors. There were people listening through the windows.

'Outside the house were five men. One of the men was very ill. The man who was ill lay on a mattress.

'"What are we going to do?" asked one man.

'"I don't know," said the second man.

'"We'll never get the mattress in there," said a third man.

'"But we must," said the fourth man. "Only Jesus can make him better."

'"I've got an idea," said the first one. He whispered his idea to the others.

'Two of the men climbed up the steps to the roof of the house. The two men took some tiles off the roof. Soon there was a big hole in the roof. The men could see Jesus through the hole.

'The men tied a rope to the mattress and lifted it on to the roof. Very carefully they lowered their friend through the hole. The man on the mattress wondered what was happening. Soon he was lying on the floor in front of Jesus.

'Jesus spoke to the man who was very ill. "Get up," he said, "pick up your mattress and go home."

'Jesus had made the man well again. He did what Jesus told him.

'Outside the house he said a very big "thank-you" to his friends,' said Mrs Jolley.

'That's what best friends would do,' said David.

9

It hurts!

 **Theme**

The story of the good Samaritan is used on so many occasions. It was an act of great kindness at personal cost.

 **Aim**

To show that true kindness means involvement

 **Bible reference**

Luke 10:25–37

'A man from Samaria then came travelling along that road. When he saw the man, he felt sorry for him and went over to him. He treated his wounds with olive oil and wine and bandaged them. Then he put him on his own donkey and took him to an inn, where he took care of him. The next morning he gave the innkeeper two silver coins and said, "Please take care of the man. If you spend more than this on him, I will pay you when I return."'

LUKE 10:33–35

A join-in prayer

Father of all,
Thank you for those who care for people.
For ambulance drivers and the police,
Thank you.
For doctors and nurses,
Thank you.
For those who care for old people,
Thank you.
For mums and dads who care for us,
Thank you.

It was playtime and the children were playing football.

'Pass it,' shouted Michael.

'Over here,' shouted James.

Joshua kicked the ball hard to James. Nathan tried to get the ball at the same time as James. They ran into each other. James fell over on the playground.

'Ow,' yelled James. The others didn't take any notice of him. They left James on the ground. David ran past James.

'Get up,' shouted David.

'I can't,' said James. 'My leg hurts.'

'Don't be a baby, James,' said Michael.

Sam went over to James. Sam went to Mrs Jolley, who was on playground duty. 'Mrs Jolley,' said Sam, 'James has hurt himself. Please come and see.'

Mrs Jolley washed James' knee and put a plaster on it.

At the end of play, Mrs Jolley asked the children to sit on the story mat.

'Jesus once told a story about a man who went on a journey. He was walking by himself along a lonely road. Suddenly some men jumped out from behind a rock. They knocked the man over. They stole all his money. They left him lying in the road. He was badly hurt.

'A little later, he heard footsteps. Now, he thought, someone would help him. "Please help me," he begged. But the footsteps just went by without stopping.

'Later still, he heard more footsteps. "Please help me," he begged. But no one answered and the footsteps went by again.

'The man lying in the road gave up hope. No one would help him.

'Then he heard a donkey trotting along the road. The donkey stopped. The donkey rider got off and came over to him. Soon the man who was hurt was bandaged and riding on the donkey. The donkey's owner walked by his side.

'As it got dark, they came to a hotel. The two men and the donkey stayed the night. In the morning the donkey's owner left some money at the hotel. "Please take care of my friend," he said.

'Jesus finished his story and asked this question. "Which of the three men was kind to the man who was robbed?"'

Mrs Jolley looked at the children.

'Can you answer the question Jesus asked?' she said.

'That's easy,' said Michael. 'The man with the donkey.'

'Yes,' said David, 'the other two just left him there.'

'If you see someone who has been hurt,' said Mrs Jolley, 'please be kind to them.'

 **Theme**

In schools today, children often make up their own class rules. These help in the smooth running of the class. Sometimes there needs to be a reminder!

 **Aim**

To show that if people want to live together happily, there must be some rules

 **Bible reference**

Exodus 20:1–17
Respect your father and your mother, and you will live a long time in the land I am giving you.
EXODUS 20:12

A join-in prayer

Loving Father,
When we are unkind
to other people,
Please forgive us.
When we only think
about ourselves,
Please forgive us.
When we want our
own way,
Please forgive us.
When we lose our tempers,
Please forgive us.

10

Rules

It had not been a good morning in Mrs Jolley's class. Emma had spilt one of the paint pots. There was red paint all over the floor. Sam had walked in the red paint. There were red footprints all round the classroom.

David and Michael had chased each other down the corridor. Sarah and Rosie had been talking to each other in assembly.

Joshua had dropped some sweet-papers in the playground. Nathan had had a fight with Hannah.

By dinner time there were not many happy faces in Mrs Jolley's classroom. Not even Mrs Jolley's!

After dinner, Mrs Jolley asked the children to sit on the story mat.

'A long time ago lived a man called Moses,' she said. 'Moses was the leader of all his people. Moses had led his people on a long journey. Moses was a man who listened to God and tried to do what God told him to do.

'One day, God told Moses to climb to the top of a high mountain. On the top of the mountain God spoke to Moses. God gave Moses some special rules for his people. These were rules to help them live happy lives. There were ten of these special rules. We call them the Ten Commandments.

'The first four rules were about how people should behave towards God. The last six rules were about how people should behave towards each other.

'Moses went down the mountain and spoke to all the people. He told them what God had said.

'You see, God knew that if people are going to live happily together, there have to be some rules. People need to remember God and they need to remember each other.

'We didn't have a good start to the day,' said Mrs Jolley. 'We didn't have a happy morning because we forgot some of our school rules.

'God's people didn't always remember to keep his rules but they did try again. And that's what we're going to do!'

 **Theme**

A good story has the right mix of happy and sad experiences. The story of Ruth has both, and is a great story with a happy ending!

 **Aim**

To show that happiness often comes from a sad experience

 **Bible reference**

The book of Ruth
Boaz answered, 'I've heard how you've helped your mother-in-law ever since your husband died. You even left your own father and mother to come and live in a foreign land among people you don't know. I pray that the Lord God of Israel will reward you for what you have done. And now that you have come to him for protection, I pray that he will bless you.'
RUTH 2:11–12

A join-in prayer

Lord God,
Thank you for the Bible.
For all the stories
about you,
Thank you.
For the stories of those
who loved you,
Thank you.
For those who wrote
these stories,
Thank you.
For making sad beginnings
into happy endings,
Thank you.

11

A sad-to-happy story

Mrs Jolley was sitting in her story chair. The children were sitting on the story mat. They were talking about stories.

'I like stories about animals,' said Rosie.

''Specially about horses,' said Emma.

'I like stories about Batman,' said David.

'What sort of stories do you like, Hannah?' asked Mrs Jolley.

Hannah thought about it for a moment. 'I like stories that have a happy ending,' said Hannah.

'So do I,' said Joshua and Nathan together.

'But some stories start sad and end happy,' said Mrs Jolley. 'The story of Ruth is like that. Ruth was a young woman. Ruth was very sad. Ruth was sad because her husband Mahlon had died.

'Ruth lived with Naomi, her husband's mother. Naomi was very sad because her son Mahlon had died.

'One day, Naomi spoke to Ruth. "I'm going home—back to my family in Bethlehem," she said. Bethlehem was a long way away. "Ruth, you must go back to your family—to your mother."

'Ruth loved Naomi. Ruth said to Naomi, "I want to stay with you. Wherever you go, I will go too. Wherever you live, I will live."

'It was very kind of Ruth to want to look after Naomi.

'They set off for Bethlehem. Naomi's family were very pleased to see them when they got there.

'Ruth went into the fields to look for corn. Ruth wanted the corn to make bread. Ruth found lots of corn.

'The man who owned the fields was very kind. He made sure Ruth found lots of corn. His name was Boaz. Boaz had heard how kind Ruth had been to Naomi.

'Boaz liked Ruth. Ruth liked Boaz. Soon Boaz married Ruth. Ruth was very happy. Naomi was very happy.

'Naomi was even happier when Ruth and Boaz had a baby. Naomi now had a little grandson,' said Mrs Jolley.

'I really, really liked that story,' said Hannah.

'The story of Ruth had a sad start,' said Mrs Jolley. 'But what sort of ending did it have?'

'A happy one,' shouted all the children.

'Now, see if you can draw some pictures of our sad-to-happy story,' said Mrs Jolley.

OTHERS

This section contains five stories which move beyond the immediate circle of friends and family, to consider the needs and deeds of others. It introduces themes of caring, sharing and consideration.

Theme

God's world is a wonderful world, even if it is raining!

Aim

To show that God keeps his promises

Bible reference

Genesis 9:9–17
God said to Noah, 'The rainbow that I have put in the sky will be my sign to you and to every living creature on earth. It will remind you that I will keep this promise for ever.'
GENESIS 9:12–13

A join-in prayer

Loving God,
Thank you for your wonderful world.
For the animals we share it with,
Thank you.
For the pets we love,
Thank you.
For hills and mountains, rivers and seas,
Thank you.
For all the wonders of nature,
Thank you.

12

Wet play with Mr Noah

It was nearly playtime. Mrs Jolley looked out of the window. It was raining hard. The rain was making big puddles outside the window.

'Oh dear,' said Mrs Jolley. 'It's going to be a wet playtime. Children, please come and sit down. We can't go out to play because of the rain.'

'Tell us a story, please,' said the children.

The children sat down in the story corner on the story mat. They sat by Mrs Jolley's story chair.

'As it's a wet day, I will tell you a story about the rain,' said Mrs Jolley. 'It's a story about Mr and Mrs Noah and their three sons. God told them to build a big ship because it was going to rain.

'It was going to rain so hard that all the puddles would turn into lakes. It was going to rain so hard that all the lakes would turn into a sea.

'God told Mr Noah to take two of every animal on his ship. There were two elephants and two mice. There were two lions and two hamsters. There were two cats and two dogs. There were two of every animal and Mr and Mrs Noah and their three sons were very busy.

'It rained for a long time and the sea got deeper and deeper. But one day, Mr and Mrs Noah looked out of the window and saw that it had stopped raining.

'Slowly the water dried up and Mr and Mrs Noah could see the tops of the mountains and hills. Then they could see trees and bushes and soon the earth looked as it had done before the rain started.

'The animals said goodbye to Mr and Mrs Noah and their three sons. The animals left Mr Noah's big ship and went off to find their new homes. Then God told Mr Noah that he would never make it rain so hard again.

'"And," said God, "to remind me of my promise, every time it rains and the sun is shining, I shall hang a rainbow in the sky."

'Mr and Mrs Noah looked up and sure enough, there was the most beautiful rainbow right over them,' said Mrs Jolley.

'Look, Mrs Jolley,' said David, 'it's stopped raining. Can we go out and play?'

'There it is,' said Sarah. 'There's the rainbow God promised.'

'Yes,' said Mrs Jolley. 'God always keeps his promises.'

And the children went out and splashed in the puddles.

 **Theme**

There are two great themes in this story—the generosity of the boy willing to hand over his packed lunch, and the concern that Jesus showed for those who followed him.

Aim

To show how by sharing we can help each other

 **Bible reference**

John 6:1–15

Andrew said, 'There is a boy here who has five small loaves of barley bread and two fish.' Jesus took the bread in his hands and gave thanks to God. Then he passed the bread to the people, and he did the same with the fish, until everyone had plenty to eat. The people ate all they wanted.

JOHN 6:9, 11, 12

A join-in prayer

Lord of all,
We have food to eat
and homes to live in.
Where there are children
who are hungry,
Please be with them.
Where there are families
who have no homes,
Please be with them.
Where there are children
who have no school to go to,
Please be with them.
Where there is anybody
who is lonely,
Please be with them.

13

Picnic in the park

'Tomorrow,' said Mrs Jolley, before the children went home, 'we are going to have a picnic in the park. Please bring your picnic lunch to school.'

The children talked about their picnic.

'I'm going to bring some crisps,' said David.

'I'm going to bring some sausage rolls,' said Sarah.

'I'm going to bring some chocolate,' said James.

'And I'm going to bring a banana,' said Hannah.

The next day the children took their picnics to school. Soon they got in a line in the playground.

'Hold hands with your partner,' said Mrs Jolley. 'And off we go.'

They walked down the road past the shops. They walked down the road to the park gates.

'Now, put all your bags under the tree,' said Mrs Jolley.

Soon there was a pile of bags under an old tree. The children played lots of games. They went to see the ducks on the pond in the park.

'Now,' said Mrs Jolley, 'it's time for lunch.'

The children went to get their bags. They sat in a circle. Joshua and his sister Rosie looked very sad.

'Please, Mrs Jolley,' said Joshua, 'we haven't got any lunch.'

'Oh dear,' said Mrs Jolley. 'You weren't at school yesterday. You didn't know about the picnic.'

'I know what we can do,' said David. 'We can all give Joshua and Rosie some of our picnic.'

'That's a lovely idea,' said Mrs Jolley. 'Thank you, David.'

Soon Joshua and Rosie had lots to eat. David gave them some of his crisps. Sarah gave them a sausage roll each. James gave them some chocolate. And Hannah shared her banana.

'We have a green story mat today,' said Mrs Jolley. 'It's called grass!

'I'm going to tell you a story about a boy who helped Jesus. Lots of people had been listening to Jesus for a long time. They were hungry and thirsty.

'Jesus asked if anyone had got any food. Andrew, one of Jesus' friends, said, "There's a boy here. He has brought a picnic with him. He wants to share it with everyone."

'Jesus took the boy's picnic and said a prayer. Soon everyone had something to eat and nobody was hungry. They weren't hungry because the boy shared his lunch.'

The children played some more games before they went back to school.

'We've had a lovely day after all,' said Joshua and Rosie.

Theme

It may be the dark, or high winds, or thunder and lightning, but most of us fear something. Jesus calmed the storm and the fears of his friends.

Aim

To show that Jesus cared for his friends—and still does

Bible reference

Mark 4:35–41

Suddenly a storm struck the lake. Waves started splashing into the boat, and it was about to sink. Jesus was in the back of the boat with his head on a pillow, and he was asleep. His disciples woke him and said, 'Teacher, don't you care that we are about to drown?' Jesus got up and ordered the wind and the waves to be quiet. The wind stopped, and everything was calm.

MARK 4:37–39

A join-in prayer

Heavenly Father,
When the wind blows hard
and we are frightened,
Please be near us.
When it is dark and we
cannot see,
Please be near us.
When the snow is deep and
the world freezes,
Please be near us.
When there is thunder
and lightning,
Please be near us.

14

Stormy weather

It was pouring with rain. The rain was running along the gutters. It was dripping off the trees. It was filling up the puddles.

The wind joined in the fun. The wind blew the rain into the children's faces. The wind blew wet leaves off the trees. The wind blew so hard, the children had to hold on tightly to their rain hats.

The children's wellies stood in little puddles. The rain dripped from the children's coats as they hung on their pegs.

By milk time the wind was blowing even harder. The wind rattled the windows. The wind rattled the doors. The wind made the trees dance.

'What a wet and windy day,' said Mrs Jolley. 'After you've finished your drinks, we will have a story.'

The children sat on the story mat.

'I think we'll have a wet and windy story,' said Mrs Jolley.

'This story starts by the side of a large lake. Jesus had spent the day talking to lots and lots of people. Everybody wanted to hear Jesus and by the evening he was very tired.

'"Let's go across the lake," said Jesus to his friends. "We'll go to the other side."

'They jumped in a boat and waved goodbye to all the people. His friends put up the sail. Soon Jesus was fast asleep.

'As the little boat got further from the shore, the wind began to blow. The wind blew harder and harder. The small waves became big waves. The big waves became very big waves. The boat began to jump up and down on the waves.

'Jesus' friends were very frightened. "The boat's filling up with water," they shouted. "We're going to drown," they shouted.

'The wind blew even harder. The waves grew even higher. But Jesus was still asleep.

'His friends went to Jesus. "Jesus, please wake up!" they shouted.

'Jesus woke up. Jesus saw how frightened everyone was. He stood up.

'"Be quiet," he said to the wind. "Be still," he said to the waves.

'The wind died down and the lake became calm.

'"There's no need to be frightened," he said to his friends. "There is never any need to be frightened when I am with you."

'Jesus and his friends got safely to the other side of the lake,' said Mrs Jolley. Outside the classroom, the wind had dropped and the rain had stopped.

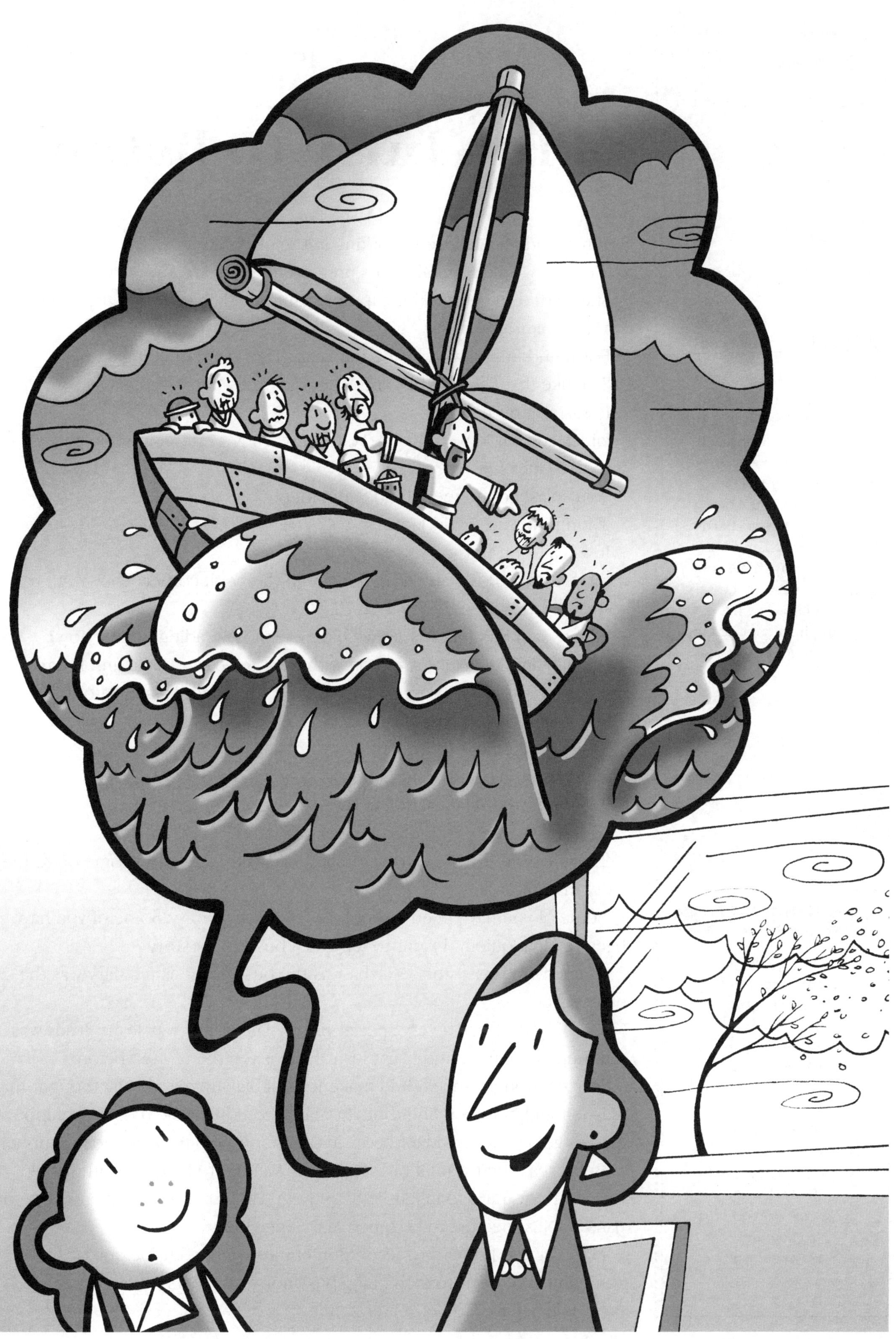

Theme

Some children's experience of being quiet is very limited. Jesus knew the value of it, often going off by himself.

Aim

To teach the need for quiet times

Bible reference

Luke 10:38–42
Martha went to Jesus and said, 'Lord, doesn't it bother you that my sister has left me to do all the work by myself? Tell her to come and help me!' The Lord answered, 'Martha, Martha! You are worried and upset about so many things, but only one thing is necessary. Mary has chosen what is best, and it will not be taken away from her.'
LUKE 10:40–42

A join-in prayer

Loving Father,
You are never too busy
to listen to us.
When we are too busy
to listen to you,
We are sorry.
When we are too busy
to help others,
We are sorry.
When we are too busy
to do things properly,
We are sorry.
When we are too busy
to be quiet,
We are sorry.

15

Too busy to listen

Hannah and Michael were working in the playhouse.

'Come on,' said Hannah, 'let's pretend to get tea ready.'

She started to get out the cups and saucers. Michael found the teapot. It was all a bit noisy.

David and Emma were using the Lego. They were building a castle.

'Not like that,' shouted David. 'The door goes here.'

It was all a bit noisy.

James and Sarah were by the water tray. They were seeing how many cups it took to fill a jug.

'You splashed me then,' said Sarah loudly.

'Didn't mean to,' said James.

It was all a bit noisy.

Joshua, Sam, Rosie and Nathan were in the book corner. They were trying to read.

'Right,' said Mrs Jolley. 'Can we have everyone reading quietly now?'

Hannah and Michael carried on with their tea party. David and Emma carried on with their Lego. Sarah splashed some more water into the jug.

Mrs Jolley spoke again.

'Quiet reading now,' she said.

'Don't want to read,' said Emma.

'Don't want to read,' said David.

'You splashed me,' shouted James to Sarah.

'Everyone, stop what you are doing,' said Mrs Jolley, 'and come on to the story mat, please.

'Some of you have been rather busy and rather noisy. Some of you have been reading quietly. I want to tell you a busy–quiet story.

'There were two sisters. Martha was the busy-noisy sister. Mary was the quiet sister.

'One day, they had a very special visitor. The visitor was Jesus. Jesus was an old friend of Martha and Mary. Jesus had visited them often before.

'Martha thought she should make Jesus a big supper. Martha thought that Mary should help her. She thought Mary should help her cook the supper. Martha got cross with Mary because she didn't help to cook the big supper.

'But Jesus didn't want a big supper. He wanted to be quiet with his old friends. He wanted to talk quietly to them. He didn't want banging pots and pans. He just needed to be quiet. Mary knew this.

'Mary sat and listened to Jesus. Sometimes we need to be quiet. Sometimes we need to stop being busy-noisy,' said Mrs Jolley.

'Now, let's have a quiet reading time.'

H T U

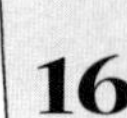

16

Please may we borrow your donkey?

Theme

There are many aspects of sharing—not just possessions but time and friendship too. The donkey's owner had no hesitation when he was told it was Jesus who wanted to borrow his donkey.

Aim

To think about sharing what we have with others

Bible reference

Luke 19:28–40

They went off and found everything just as Jesus had said. While they were untying the donkey, its owners asked, 'Why are you doing that?' They answered, 'The Lord needs it.' Then they led the donkey to Jesus.

LUKE 19:32–35

A join-in prayer

Lord God,
For sharing Jesus with us,
Thank you.
For sharing your world with us,
Thank you.
For sharing your love with us,
Thank you.

It was the last day of the Spring term'. Mrs Jolley had told the children, the day before, that they could bring in a special toy. The children helped Mrs Jolley clear up the classroom.

'Now,' said Mrs Jolley, 'you can play quietly with your toys.'

David took a Batman model out of his bag. He had a Batmobile as well.

Emma had dressed up her Barbie doll specially. She brought some other Barbie clothes as well.

Hannah had brought in a big cuddly panda. Michael had a bag of his best cars. There were lots of them.

Sam and Sarah hadn't been at school the day before. They didn't know they could bring toys.

'Can I play with one of your cars?' Sam asked Michael.

'No,' said Michael, 'they're mine.'

'Can I see your Barbie?' asked Sarah.

'No,' said Emma, 'she's mine.'

Sam went over to David. Sam saw David's Batman and Batmobile.

'Can I play with your Batman?' asked Sam.

'No,' said David, 'he's mine.'

Sarah held out her arms to Hannah's big cuddly panda.

'Can I cuddle your panda?' asked Sarah.

'No,' said Hannah, 'he's mine.'

'Please come and sit on the story mat,' said Mrs Jolley. 'We don't seem to be very good at sharing today. I'm going to tell you a sharing story. It happened just before Easter a long time ago.

'Jesus wanted to ride into the city of Jerusalem. He needed a donkey. Jesus sent two of his friends to fetch him a donkey.

'They went into a village. They saw a donkey tied to a post. The man who owned the donkey was standing there.

'"Please may we borrow your donkey?" asked Jesus' friends. "You see, Jesus needs it."

'"Yes," said the donkey's owner. "I am very happy to share my donkey with Jesus."

'Jesus' friends took the donkey to Jesus. Jesus rode the donkey into the city of Jerusalem. It was the first Palm Sunday,' said Mrs Jolley, 'when the owner shared his donkey with Jesus. And now back to your tables, please.'

Michael went off and was soon sharing his cars with Sam. And Emma let Sarah dress her Barbie doll.

FESTIVALS

Some of the happiest times in school relate to special times or festivals—not just Christmas and Harvest but Easter and Creation as well. Easter is often considered a difficult festival to teach to young children. Here are three stories to help to introduce the Easter message. There is a suggestion for participation in Harvest celebrations and also a reminder of Creation.

 **Theme**

The birth of Jesus is taught by relating it to the birth of a child today—from the known to the unknown.

 **Aim**

To introduce the Christmas story

 **Bible reference**

Luke 2:1–7
Mary was engaged to Joseph and travelled with him to Bethlehem. She was soon going to have a baby, and while they were there, she gave birth to her firstborn son. She dressed him in baby clothes and laid him on a bed of hay, because there was no room for them in the inn.
LUKE 2:5–7

A join-in prayer

Dear Lord,
Thank you for Jesus' birthday.
For the love of Mary and Joseph,
Thank you.
For the donkey that carried Mary to the stable,
Thank you.
For the kindness of the innkeeper,
Thank you.
For all that Jesus' birthday means to us today,
Thank you.

17

Happy birthday to you

Sarah came running into school with a big smile. Sarah saw Mrs Jolley sitting by her table. Sarah ran over to Mrs Jolley.

'My auntie's had a new baby,' she said. 'It's a little boy and we're going to see him after school.'

'That's wonderful,' said Mrs Jolley. 'That makes today a very special day. I think we'll start today with a story.'

The children sat down on the story mat.

'Sarah has got something very special to tell us,' said Mrs Jolley.

Sarah stood by Mrs Jolley's story chair.

'My Auntie Jane's had a new baby,' she told all the children. 'It's a little boy and he's called Edward and we're going to see him!'

'Thank you, Sarah,' said Mrs Jolley.

'Baby Edward was born in the hospital. I'm going to tell you a story about a baby who was born in a stable. That's a funny place to be born, but this baby was born a long time ago and there weren't any hospitals.

'The baby's mummy was called Mary and she was married to Joseph. They had been on a long journey and were a long way from home. It was the time for Mary's baby to be born.

'Joseph tried hard to find somewhere for them to stay. But there was no room anywhere.

'A kind man told Joseph that they could use his stable. It was dry and there was a lot of warm straw.

'Joseph took a blanket off the donkey Mary had been riding. Mary lay on the blanket and soon the baby was born.

'"Mary," said Joseph with a big smile, "we have a lovely baby boy."

'Mary and Joseph were very happy. There was a manger in the stable. A manger is where food for the animals is put. Joseph cleaned the manger and put the baby in it. Soon the baby was fast asleep.

'"What shall we call our baby?" whispered Joseph.

'"His name is Jesus," said Mary very quietly. "That is the name God wants us to call him."

'And Jesus grew up to be a very special person indeed,' said Mrs Jolley.

'Now, I think it would be a good idea if everyone made a card for Sarah to take to Edward.'

cm

Theme

The shepherds and the angels all had an important part to play in the Christmas story. The fear of the shepherds turns to joy as they find the words of the angel coming true.

Aim

To show how everyone in the Christmas story was important

Bible reference

Luke 2:8–20

That night in the fields near Bethlehem some shepherds were guarding their sheep. All at once an angel came down to them from the Lord, and the brightness of the Lord's glory flashed around them. The shepherds were frightened. But the angel said, 'Don't be afraid! I have good news for you, which will make everyone happy. This very day in King David's home town a Saviour was born for you. He is Christ the Lord.'
LUKE 2:8–11

A join-in prayer

Father God,
For the story of Christmas,
Thank you.
For the message
of the angels,
Thank you.
For the happiness
of the shepherds,
Thank you.
For the love of Mary
and Joseph,
Thank you.

Shepherds and angels

There were cards to make. There were presents to think about. There were pretty decorations up in the classroom.

There were only a few more days before school finished and the Christmas holidays began. All the children were getting very excited.

'Next week,' said Mrs Jolley, when the children were quietly sitting on the story mat, 'we are going to have a nativity play. Can anyone tell me what a nativity play is?'

Emma put up her hand. 'It's a play about Jesus being born,' she said.

'Quite right, Emma,' said Mrs Jolley. 'The play tells the story of when Jesus was born in Bethlehem. Our class will be the shepherds and the angels.'

'Don't want to be an angel,' said Michael, loud enough for Mrs Jolley to hear.

'Michael, I think you would make a good shepherd,' said Mrs Jolley.

Michael looked happier.

Sarah looked puzzled and put her hand up. 'Please, Mrs Jolley, what's an angel?' she asked.

'And what do they wear?' asked Hannah.

'They wear nightie things,' said Nathan. The other children laughed. 'Well, they did at my play school,' he said.

Mrs Jolley smiled. 'When Jesus was born in the stable in Bethlehem,' she said, 'something very wonderful happened. On the hills, outside Bethlehem, some shepherds looked after their sheep. The shepherds always stayed with their sheep. They were there during the day and during the night. One of the shepherds stayed awake at night to watch out for wild animals.

'On the night that Jesus was born, the shepherd who was awake had a big surprise. One moment it was quiet. He could see the stars and hear the other shepherds snoring. The next minute the sky was full of angels singing. One angel spoke to him.

'"Don't be afraid," said the angel. "I've got some very good news for you. Jesus has been born in Bethlehem."

'By this time all the shepherd's friends were awake. The choir of angels flew away, still singing. You see, the angels were the first carol singers.

'The shepherds were very excited. "Let's go and find the baby," they said.

'One shepherd stayed to look after the sheep. The others ran as fast as they could down the hill into Bethlehem. They found baby Jesus as the angel had promised. On their way back up the hill, the shepherds sang just as the angels had done. Angels,' said Mrs Jolley, 'are God's messengers. We think they look a bit like us but they probably have wings.

'Now, who wants to be a shepherd and who wants to be an angel?'

'I want to be an angel,' said Michael.

Theme

Christmas, in the eyes of so many people, is a time of receiving presents. The gifts of the wise men had great significance to the life of Jesus.

Aim

To teach about Jesus through the gifts of the wise men

Bible reference

Matthew 2:1–12

When the [wise] men went into the house and saw the child with Mary, his mother, they knelt down and worshipped him. They took out their gifts of gold, frankincense, and myrrh and gave them to him.
MATTHEW 2:11

A join-in prayer

Loving Father,
You have given us so much.
For the wonderful world
we live in,
Thank you.
For all those who
look after us,
Thank you.
For the love of our
families and friends,
Thank you.
For Jesus, your present
to us,
Thank you.

19

Presents

It was the first day back at school after the Christmas holidays. The children were talking about their Christmas presents.

'I had the Man United football strip,' said Michael.

'I got a pram for my best doll,' said Sarah.

'I had a watch,' said Joshua.

'And I've got a…'

'Children,' said Mrs Jolley, 'please come and sit down.'

The children stopped talking and sat down on the story mat.

'I wonder if anyone can guess what I had for Christmas?' asked Mrs Jolley. 'If you look hard, you might be able to see it.'

All the children stared at Mrs Jolley. Hannah put up her hand.

'I think you've got a new necklace,' she said.

'Well done,' said Mrs Jolley. 'Hannah is right. My husband gave me a lovely gold chain.'

And Mrs Jolley lifted the chain and showed the children how it shone.

'My gold chain reminded me of some special presents. Do you remember, before Christmas, we thought about Jesus being born?

'When he was a little bit older, he had some rather unusual visitors. They had come a very long way to see Jesus. These men were very clever. They were so clever, they used to tell their king what he should do. We usually call them the three wise men.

'When they found Jesus, they each gave him a present. The first wise man gave him some gold. Gold is the most precious metal and it used to be given to kings.

'The second wise man gave Jesus some perfume called frankincense. Frankincense is used in some churches to make a nice smell.

'The third wise man gave Jesus some myrrh. Myrrh is a special ointment which is put on the body when someone in a hot country dies.

'These were rather strange presents for baby Jesus. But, you see, Jesus is a king and so he was given gold. Jesus is God's Son whom we worship. And Jesus died on the special day we call Good Friday.

'So perhaps they were the right Christmas presents for Jesus,' said Mrs Jolley.

'Now, it's time you told me about your best present.'

20

Special times

Theme

Special times are those moments that are looked back to and treasured. The special time that Jesus spent with his friends in the upper room is something that Christians look back to and treasure.

Aim

To learn about the Last Supper in the Easter story

Bible reference

Luke 22:7–20

Jesus took some bread in his hands and gave thanks for it. He broke the bread and handed it to his apostles. Then he said, 'This is my body, which is given for you. Eat this as a way of remembering me!' After the meal he took [a] cup of wine in his hands. Then he said, 'This is my blood. It is poured out for you, and with it God makes his new agreement.'

LUKE 22:19–20

A join-in prayer

Father God,
Thank you for all the
special times we have.
For good times with friends,
Thank you.
For good times at school,
Thank you.
For good times with
mum and dad,
Thank you.
For good times with you,
Thank you.

The children were sitting on the story mat. Mrs Jolley was reading some poems.

'Can we have *Special Times*, please?' asked Rosie. *Special Times* was one of the poems the children liked best.

'Please, Mrs Jolley,' said the others.

'Yes,' said Mrs Jolley, 'I'll read *Special Times* and then we'll have a story.'

This is the poem that Mrs Jolley read to the children.

A story read by mum or dad,
A great big hug when I've been bad.
Watching caterpillars climb,
That's a funny special time.

Christmas presents by the tree,
Favourite programmes on TV.
Playing in the mud and slime,
That's a messy special time!

Eating lollies in the park,
Watching stars when it gets dark.
Going to the pantomime,
That's a really special time.

Holding hands with my best friend,
Playing games like 'Let's pretend',
Singing favourite nursery rhymes,
These are all my Special Times.

'And now,' said Mrs Jolley, 'a "special time" story.

'Jesus had nearly finished what God his father wanted him to do. It was nearly time for Jesus to say goodbye.

'It was the day before Good Friday. Jesus died on Good Friday. Jesus wanted a last special time with his friends. He chose to have a meal with them.

'Two of his friends, Peter and John, went to get everything ready. When it was ready, Jesus sat down at the table. His friends were all there with him.

'Jesus picked up some bread. He broke it into small pieces. All his friends ate a piece.

'"Remember me when you eat bread," said Jesus.

'Jesus passed a cup of wine to his friends. All his friends drank a little wine.

'"Remember me when you drink wine," said Jesus.

'People who love Jesus have done that ever since,' said Mrs Jolley. 'They have always remembered this special time Jesus had with his friends. They have remembered it by eating bread and by drinking wine.

'We call this special time Holy Communion,' said Mrs Jolley. 'It is the special time Jesus gave to us.'

Theme

Some children are far better than others at offering help, at seeing what needs to be done. Jesus, Son of God, shows by his example in this story what really matters.

Aim

To show how Jesus willingly did the lowest job

Bible reference

John 13:1–11

During the meal Jesus got up, removed his outer garment, and wrapped a towel around his waist. He put some water into a large bowl. Then he began washing his disciples' feet and drying them with the towel he was wearing.
JOHN 13:4–5

A join-in prayer

Loving Father,
Thank you for Jesus.
For the way he cares about us,
And shows us how to care.
When we haven't been helpful,
We are sorry.
When we think about ourselves first,
We are sorry.
When we forget to say "sorry",
We are sorry.

21

Feet first

It had been a busy morning in Mrs Jolley's class. Joshua and Hannah had been cutting coloured shapes. There were pieces of paper on the chairs. There were pieces of paper on the floor. There were even pieces of paper in Joshua's hair!

Michael and Rosie had been working in the sand tray. There was sand on the table. There was sand on the floor. There was sand on their clothes.

Emma and Nathan had been colouring some pictures. There were wax crayons on the table. One crayon rolled on to the floor. The crayon broke into lots of pieces.

'Children,' said Mrs Jolley, 'stop what you are doing, please. It is time to tidy up. Put everything back where you got it from.'

Joshua and Hannah carried on talking to each other.

'I'm not going to pick up all those bits,' said Joshua.

Michael and Rosie went to wash their hands. They didn't brush up the sand that had fallen on the floor.

Emma and Nathan put their pictures in their trays. They left crayons lying on the table. They left the broken crayon lying on the floor.

The school bell rang for lunch time. The children went and had their lunch.

When Joshua and Hannah came back, they were surprised. Their pieces of paper were still on the floor. Michael and Rosie were surprised. The sand they had spilt was still on the floor. Emma and Nathan were surprised. Their crayons had not been put back in the box.

Mrs Jolley asked the children to sit on the story mat.

'We had a busy morning this morning,' she said. 'You worked with the sand, and with the scissors and with the crayons. But no one put anything away. You all left it for someone else to do.

'I want to tell you a story about Jesus. It happened when Jesus had his special meal with his friends. In those days, everyone wore sandals on their feet. The roads were very dusty when it was hot. The roads were very muddy when it was wet. And everybody's feet got very, very dirty.

'Jesus put a towel round himself. He filled a basin with some water. Jesus knelt on the floor. He washed the feet of all his friends, one by one. He dried them carefully on the towel. Jesus, who was God's Son, did this for his friends. He didn't think he was too great to wash their feet. He just did it.'

Mrs Jolley looked at the children. The children didn't look at Mrs Jolley. It was quiet for a moment.

'Sorry we didn't clear up our cutting-out,' said Joshua.

'Sorry about the sand,' said Rosie.

'And sorry about the crayons,' said Emma and Nathan together.

22

Mary's Easter garden

Theme

Like Christmas, Easter can be lost in the wrapping paper of eggs and bunnies! Mary shows the true meaning—*Jesus is alive!*

Aim

To share the happiness of Easter

Bible reference

John 20:1–18

Jesus asked Mary, 'Why are you crying? Who are you looking for?' She thought he was the gardener and said, 'Sir, if you have taken his body away, please tell me, so I can go and get him.' Then Jesus said to her, 'Mary!' She turned and said to him, 'Rabboni.' The Aramaic word 'Rabboni' means 'Teacher'.
JOHN 20:15–16

A join-in prayer

Father of all,
For the happiness of Easter,
We thank you.
For all the signs of
new life at Easter,
We thank you.
For Jesus coming
alive again,
We thank you.
For our friendship
with him,
We thank you.

The sun was shining as the children came to school. There were only a few fluffy clouds. The birds were singing. It was a beautiful Spring day.

'Let's have a look at our bulbs,' said Emma.

Emma and Hannah skipped over to the school garden. They had planted the bulbs before Christmas. 'Look,' said Emma, 'they're daffodils now.' The bulbs had grown into lovely yellow daffodils.

The whistle went in the playground. Emma and Hannah ran back and lined up with the others in Mrs Jolley's class.

'Joshua,' said Mrs Jolley, 'please take the register to the office. The rest of you, come and sit on the story mat, please.'

The children sat down quietly and waited for Joshua.

'Today,' said Mrs Jolley, 'we're going to make something very special. Today we're going to make an Easter garden.'

'Does it have Easter eggs in it?' asked Rosie.

'I've got three Easter eggs at home,' said Nathan.

'No,' said Mrs Jolley, smiling, 'an Easter garden doesn't have Easter eggs in it. I'll tell you the story of the first Easter garden. It's a story about Jesus and some of his friends. It's a sad-to-happy story.

'You see, on Good Friday we remember that Jesus died. On the first Good Friday, his friends thought they would never see Jesus again.

'After Jesus died, his friends put him into a grave. It was like a small cave. They put Jesus into the cave and rolled a big stone in front of it. They were very sad when they left him there and went home.

'On Easter Sunday, Mary, a special friend of Jesus, went to the cave. When Mary got there, the stone had been rolled away. Mary started to cry. She loved Jesus very much and Jesus had gone. Mary was very sad.

'Then someone spoke to her. "Why are you crying?"

'Mary was crying so much, she couldn't see who it was. "Please tell me where Jesus is," she begged.

'"MARY." It was Jesus.

'Mary blinked back her tears. It really was Jesus. Jesus was alive after all.

'"Go and tell my other friends you have seen me," said Jesus.

'Mary rushed out of the Easter garden. She ran as fast as she could. A sad day had become a really happy one,' said Mrs Jolley.

'So what do you think we might have in our Easter garden?'

'A cave,' said Michael.

'And some flowers,' said Sarah.

'And a Mary and a Jesus,' said James.

'And they're both looking happy!' said Rosie.

23

Harvest

Theme

So much is taken for granted today as we find all the things we need in a supermarket. At Harvest time we are reminded that everything comes from God and from the hard work of many people. There is so much for which to say 'thank you'.

Aim

To make a whole-class contribution to a Harvest assembly

Bible reference

Psalm 65:9–13
Wherever your footsteps touch the earth, a rich harvest is gathered. Desert pastures blossom, and mountains celebrate. Meadows are filled with sheep and goats; valleys overflow with grain and echo with joyful songs.
PSALM 65:11–13

A join-in prayer

Great God our Father,
You have made a beautiful world for us to live in.
Help us to look after it.
For farmers who grow food for us,
Please be with them.
For those who look after animals,
Please be with them.
For those who have dangerous jobs,
Please be with them.
For those people who have bad harvests and are hungry,
Please be with them.

'Next week,' said Mrs Jolley, 'is our Harvest Festival. We shall have a special school assembly. Harvest is a thank-you time. A thank-you for all the things that God has given us. If you can think of some of them, I'll write a list.'

The children suggested bananas, apples, potatoes, burgers and fish fingers.

'We should say "thank you" for food,' said Mrs Jolley. 'But what about other things?'

The children thought of dogs, cats, tortoises and grandads!

'We're getting a lovely long list,' said Mrs Jolley. 'Now we need to think about the assembly. In the Bible there are 150 songs which we call psalms. I'm going to read from Psalm 65. Shut your eyes. Now try to see the picture the words are painting.'

Wherever your footsteps touch the earth, a rich harvest is gathered. Desert pastures blossom, and mountains celebrate. Meadows are filled with sheep and goats; valleys overflow with grain and echo with joyful songs.

'What did you see in that picture?'

'I saw lots and lots of sheep,' said Hannah. 'I saw lots of corn growing,' said David. 'And I saw lots of people, all being happy!' said Rosie.

Everyone laughed at what Rosie said.

'Well done,' said Mrs Jolley. 'Now we are going to paint that picture. We'll make a great big frieze showing the hills and valleys.

'Everyone can make his or her own sheep and then stick it on the frieze.'

'Can I make a horse?' asked Hannah.

'Yes, I think we'll put some horses and cows on our picture too,' said Mrs Jolley.

David, Sarah and Joshua helped Mrs Jolley make the frieze.

'It will have to be a really big one,' said Mrs Jolley. 'We shall put it up in the Big Hall for the assembly.'

David, Sarah and Joshua finished the frieze. Everyone came and stuck his or her own sheep on it. There were some horses and cows.

'There's no people,' said Sam.

'Well done, Sam,' said Mrs Jolley. 'You are going to be the people. In the assembly you are all going to stand in front of the frieze. Everyone will say "thank you" for one thing.

'So we'll start with David saying, "Thank you for bananas." Then when everyone has finished, I shall read those verses again. And you will be the people who make the joyful songs.'

And that's what happened. A week later, the Harvest Festival assembly went very well indeed.

Theme

Everyone has a part to play in creation—sometimes good and sometimes bad. This story helps to celebrate creation and to show that it is ongoing.

Aim

To show how we all have a part to play in creating things

Bible reference

Genesis 1:1—2:4
God said, 'Now we will make humans, and they will be like us. We will let them rule the fish, the birds, and all other living creatures.' So God created humans to be like himself; he made men and women.
GENESIS 1:26–27

A join-in prayer

Lord of creation,
For the wonderful world
we live in,
Thank you.
For light to work in and
darkness to sleep in,
Thank you.
For water that keeps
your world alive,
Thank you.
For food that helps us grow,
Thank you.

24

Start at the beginning

Half of Mrs Jolley's class were painting. Emma was staring at the big sheet of paper. David was looking at the paints. Sarah was splashing the brush in the water pot.

'Well, come on then,' said Mrs Jolley. 'Let's make a start.'

'I don't know where to begin,' said Emma.

'What colour should I use?' asked David.

'Do I use a thick brush or a thin one?' asked Sarah.

'I think we'd better talk about it,' said Mrs Jolley. 'Leave all the paint things and come over to the story mat,' she said.

'I'm going to tell you a story…' said Mrs Jolley.

'About painting!' said David.

'No,' said Mrs Jolley, 'but it is about making things. A long, long,time ago, God thought he would make the world. At the time, everything was dark. It wasn't just dark. It was so dark you couldn't see anything at all.

'So God made some light, which he called "day". The darkness that was left he called "night".

'He made some sky with fluffy clouds. Into the sky he put the sun and the moon. The sun shone in the day and the moon shone in the night.

'God looked at the sea. It was everywhere. God told the sea to move over a bit. And there was the land. Quickly he filled the land with plants and bushes and trees. Green was a good colour. Lots of the world looked green now.

'But there was still something missing.

'"Animals," thought God. "We must have lots of animals."

'Soon there were birds flying everywhere. Soon there were fish swimming. Soon there were sheep and cows and dogs and cats and horses and caterpillars and zebras and…

'Can you tell me some more animals?' asked Mrs Jolley.

The children suggested camels, pigs, monkeys and hamsters.

'But,' said Mrs Jolley, 'God hadn't finished. Who have we forgotten?'

'US,' shouted Emma. And everyone laughed.

'Quite right,' said Mrs Jolley, smiling. 'Us. God made us to look after all the birds, the fish and the animals.

'But, you know, I think God thought a lot about what he was going to do before he started. It's a little bit like your painting. You must think about it before you start,' said Mrs Jolley.

'Now, why don't you paint a part of the story I've just told you?'

'I'm going to paint the fish,' said Emma.

'I'm going to paint a lion,' said David.

'And I'm going to paint us!' said Sarah.